GRACE:
God's Redemption At Christ's Expense

Acknowledgement:
Thanks and appreciation goes to my wife,
Alicia Contreras Rogers, for being my
encouragement and willing proof reader.
....
A special 'thank you' goes to Dr David M Ford.
Without your efforts I would not have written my
original paper on 'grace.'

Contents:

GRACE:
God's Redemption At Christ's Expense

Dr David J Rogers

CreateSpace
http://www.createspace.com

1 | GRACE

"The grace of the Lord Jesus Christ, and the love of God, and the communion of the Holy Ghost, be with you all. Amen."
- II Corinthians 13.14 KJV

The grace of the Lord Jesus Christ is the starting place for a relationship with the God of the Judeo-Christian Bible. If it was not for the acts of Jesus' love and kindness to us, we could have no relationship with God at all. Grace starts with him.

Someone once took the word *"grace"* and made it into an anagram – where each letter in a word represents a word or phrase.

GRACE: God's Riches At Christ's Expense

When I first heard the word "grace" used in this manner, I puzzled over it. It did not seem to fit. According to the Bible, God did not give us Jesus that we might be rich; although He did give all things to enjoy. God gave us Jesus that we might have a relationship, a proper relationship, with Him. God was not out to make us rich. God was out to make us have a relationship with Him.

Jesus used the parable of the prodigal son[1] to show us God's heart toward us. God loves us so much that He is willing to let us run off and do our own thing, whatsoever seems good to us, but He still looks for our return. In the parable, the prodigal son comes to his senses and realizes that servants in his father's house are treated better than he was living – among the pigs, sharing their food. As the son nears his father's house, his father spies him while he is still a long way off and runs to his son, falls on his neck with kisses, orders his servants to bring a robe, a ring, and the fatted calf. His son has returned home.

---

[1] Luke 15.11-32

This is the image of the love and grace our father in Heaven has for us. We may have chosen to take what is ours and live a life that is pleasing to us. We may have squandered everything that was entrusted to us. We may feel we are less than servants in our father's eyes, no longer worthy to be called family. We may not even want to come to God because of our shame of where we are and what we have done. God does not care about that. He knows where you are, what you have done, yet He is waiting and looking everyday for our return.

And yet while a long way off – still smelling of pigs and our world travels, He sees us coming. Just as we are hoping for mercy and to be at least a servant in His house, He forgives us of everything. He calls for the signet ring showing everyone we are fully family. He calls for new clothes and dresses us in His best. He calls for a celebration, a party in our name, for us, about us, because in His eyes we were once dead and now we are alive.

This is only possible through the grace of the Lord Jesus Christ. Grace, then, is not God's riches at Christ's expense, but God's redemption at Christ's expense.

GRACE: God's Redemption At Christ's Expense

In the parable, the returning son was not made rich by his father. He was returned to right position in the family, to the right status by his father. He was redeemed, revalued, re-judged and remade family by his father.

That is what Jesus did for us. He gave us an opportunity to be redeemed, revalued, re-judged, and remade family, by his taking our place in judgment.

Some have said, "But, I didn't ask for him to die for me." He did. It was a free gift to you. The price was paid for you. You were not asked.

A gift is something you receive without having to ask for it. If you asked for it, it would not be a free gift. It would be an answered request. A gift is where someone cared for you so much they gave out of their caring for you.

God loved you so much that He gave His only begotten son that you might live. Jesus loved you so much that he willingly took your place in judgment and laid down his life in your place. Since it is a gift, all you have to do is accept it and receive it. Once receiving it, you can begin walking in a right relationship with God. If you have accepted this grace as yours, you need only to walk in it and learn about it.

Grace, in this instance, is more than a word. It is an act given as a gift. I did not know this for many years. My understanding of grace was skewed, so I began to look into *grace* as a word and as an act. I discovered grace was far more than

I imagined. Its value is far more than all the wealth of the Earth; than the universe.

I discovered that grace really was God's redemption at Christ's expense. He valued me that much. He values you that much too.

2 | What is Grace?

Whenever I ask myself a question about a phrase or word, I have the tendency to pull out my four inch thick dictionary and research the origin of a word. I will give a quick review of the different long English definitions listed under the word. But, what I really spend time reviewing is the origin of where we got the word in the first place. So I looked at the word "grace," from the view point of Webster's New Twentieth Century Dictionary – Unabridged.

Our English word grace comes from the Latin word *gratia*, which means favor, esteem, or kindness. *Gratia* comes from the Latin word *gratus*, which means pleasing or agreeable. Looking at Webster's definition of grace, it can be said that grace is favor, esteem, or kindness that is received from another.

Grace in this form comes in many different varieties. Grace could be the favor one gives you when you are in need or want, or grace could be a gift someone wanted to give you simply because they wanted to give you a gift. It made them happy to give the gift. They hoped that by you receiving the gift you, too, would be made happy – blessed.

When God gives us grace, He is giving us gifts from His favor; blessing us with His kindness or mercy, blessing us with His goods or provision, blessing us with talents or abilities beyond our normal ability to do or perform. Graces or gifts in this manner are limitless and as varied as there are people on the face of the Earth.

How easily I have mistaken His grace over the years. As a youth, "saying" grace over my meal would have been inappropriate. But, asking for God's grace or thanking God for His grace through provision of the meal would have been appropriate.

In the past I have misunderstood what was given as a gift to be as normal. I unrealistically expected what was normal and easy for me to be normal and easy for everyone else. I was not alone in this. Others I have known have thought the same thing. Why were things that came easy to one person not as easy for another? I could do it. Why could they not do it? Grace. Not everyone is graced with the same gifts and abilities or graced to the same purpose.

Still others have accepted abilities and favor as entitlements due because they 'were', misusing the gift that was given them, taking in vain things they should have seen as gifted or granted. Perhaps we should see these graces as gifts, free-will gifts from God, given for a purpose.

Some have demanded, cried out for gifts, abilities, callings, or purpose other than what they had or what they had seen others have. A gift demanded is not a gift. It is a payment or extortion; perhaps even covetousness. A gift given freely cannot be demanded or taken by force. Grace being favor, a free gift by choice of the giver, could not be anything other than the free generosity, esteem, or kindness of one to another. In this application, God giving graces to us.

The Bible confirms God gives grace. The word *"grace"* is used 170 times in the King James Version of the Holy Bible. The importance in the meaning of the word is in its use.

There have been some excellent scholars of the Bible. These scholars have made some excellent biblical references available to see how the words were used in the Bible.

Vine's Complete Expository Dictionary of Old and New Testament Words tells us the word *"grace"* comes from the Greek word *charis*. The subjective definition is *"on the part of the bestower, the friendly disposition from which the kindly act proceeds, graciousness, loving-kindness, and goodwill generally."*

The New Strong's Dictionary of Hebrew and Greek Words shows us that χαριζ (charis) is defined as "the divine influence upon the heart, and its reflection in the life – acceptable, benefit, favor, gift, joy, liberality, pleasure, thank."

Grace, whether in English, Latin, or Greek, would be the gifting of favor or esteem upon someone. Effectively, you liked them, so you wanted to do something nice for them and gifted them. The gift does not have to be anything specific. It is a gift. In our case with God, He gifted us with favor (grace) and that expressed in the life, cross, burial, and resurrection of Jesus Christ. We did not deserve the gift. The gift was given out of His grace, His kindness toward us.

Grace was also used to recognize a gifting or talent or charisma someone had. People with a peculiar ability that seems to require minimal effort to perform have been referred to as having been "gifted" or "graced" or having the "grace" for doing a thing, or exuding a kindness and disposition of friendliness, charity, or warmth of personality. Grace can be seen as an innate ability or affinity to do something with apparent ease.

The grace of Jesus Christ speaks to another type of grace; a grace that is a free gift from someone who is able and willing to someone who is not. A grace of God was expressed in Jesus that while we were yet separate from God, still in sin, Jesus loved us so much as to see us as sheep without a shepherd, lost and dying without a savior. Jesus so loved us that his expression of grace was to take our judgment that we might live with God.

The Greek word *charis* also implies a gifting from someone who is in a higher position to someone who is in a lower position. Jesus, as the Son of God gave from that higher position to us. It was within his ability, his power, to give us the gift of life through a right relationship with God, the Father.

This singular act that God performed through Jesus is without comparison; a spiritual act carried out in the flesh, once for all.

Grace is still many things, but more than all these others things, grace is God's redemption at Christ's expense.

3 | God: The "G" of grace

When we look at grace, why is God's grace so important? To really know the answer, you must know who God is.

The Judeo-Christian Bible was written to an audience that already knew who God was. They had grown up with Him as part of their lives, their everyday culture. He was every facet of their being. As they knew, God called the descendants of Abraham, Isaac, and Jacob to serve Him only. He had separated Abraham and Isaac and Jacob individually to Himself, to walk before Him. He called their descendents to serve Him, and through their descendents all the nations of the Earth would be blessed. So, the Israelites, the Israeli, the Jews knew who God was and is. The rest of the world did not have that same life education.

In the three hundred years after the flood, from Noah to Abram, there had come into the minds of Man to name and follow after perceived powers in the Earth. They referred to them as mighty ones, as deities, as gods.

The English word "god" comes from the Middle English, Anglo-Saxon, Goth word *god* or *godd*. This word meant deity and someone with divine nature.

In the Greek the word is *theos*. In the Hebrew the word is *el*. The base meaning of the words *el* or *theos* is one who has strength, might, power, great, is strong.

Joseph Campbell's[2] work in researching myth showed there have been many who were called gods. Why is the Judeo-Christian god different? What makes receiving grace from the Judeo-Christian god so special?

---

[2] Joseph John Campbell, 1904-1987, self proclaimed mythologist

It is the very nature of whom He is and how He made Himself known to Man that makes Him, the Judeo-Christian god, different.

In Genesis 1.1, the Judeo-Christian god introduces Himself as *Elohim.* "In the beginning God (*Elohim*) created the heavens and the earth." [KJV]

This is an important introduction of Himself. *Elohim* is the plural of the Hebrew word *eloah* (deity), which comes from the root word *el* (strength, mighty, power). *Elohim* could be defined as "gods" or as powers. As *elohim* is used in Genesis 1.1, it implies that the one creating the heavens and earth encompassed all power or might in Himself.

This upsets all of the polytheistic religions and apologists. Polytheistic religions of the Sumerians, the Babylonians, the Egyptians, the Greeks, and the Romans acknowledge there are many gods, or many powers or mighty ones. The god of the Judeo-Christian Bible states there is only one god in whom all power exists, just one creator of all that is. He does not acknowledge any other gods as equals in pantheon or in power. He calls them dead, lifeless creations of Man. He acknowledges that He alone is the living and true GOD.

In Genesis 2.4, *Elohim* further defines who He is. "These are the generations of the heavens and of the earth when they were created, in the day that the LORD God made the earth and the heavens." [KJV]

In Genesis 2.4, God further defined Himself as *YHWH Elohim*. The word *yhwh* implies self-existence. It comes from the root Hebrew word *hâyâh*, which means to exist, to be. The implication God makes is that He is the self-existent, no beginning-no ending one in whom all powers exist and the creator of all things that have been made. This is His suppositional truth. This is His basis for everything else He says or does.

The God of the Judeo-Christian Bible says He created all things that were made, the Earth, and the heavens. He acknowledges no other partners or partnerships in His supremacy.

In a world of people saying there are many gods, many powers, or their god is best, the God of the Judeo-Christian Bible says those other gods do not matter and will burn in His judgment of them. God demands sole recognition of Himself as the One God of all Heaven and Earth, God above all other gods.

Bible translators have recognized His uniqueness in the world, in history, and have used the convention of using "God" in the place of *elohim* and "LORD" in the place of *YHWH* when these two words specifically reference the God of the Bible. Using Lord God was an easier explanation, a short form, and a way to honor the name of the Judeo-Christian God; to honor Him by making even His name holy and sacred.

So, why is God's grace so important to us?

The creator of heaven, earth, and all things that exist desires to give us favor. The one in whom all power exists wants to extend to us "the friendly disposition from which the kindly act proceeds, graciousness, loving-kindness, and goodwill," because we were made in His image and likeness, to be with Him.

You could have no better benefactor, no better patron, no better ally, no better friend, and no better parent than He who rules the heavens and the earth, and He extends to us His free gift of grace.

This is important. This free gift of grace explains many of the things God has done and reasons why God has done the things He has done for those that love Him and are called according to His purposes.

This free gift of grace explains His temperance toward us, His patience, His protection of us, His blessing of us, His other gifts to us, His long suffering of all our foolish ways.

4 | Redemption: The "R" of Grace

In the book of Genesis, we read how God made the heavens and the Earth, and all the things that are on the Earth. And, we read where God made Man after His own image and likeness, and then He breathed life into Man. Man was to be the children of God and to be like Him. He gave Adam specific tasks and together they were to carry them out. God did not need Man. He wanted Man to share in all things with Him.

As we read through the rest of Genesis, we see how Man sins, separates his will from God's.

The English word "sin" comes from the Anglo-Saxon word *synn* or *sin*, which means evil or wickedness. Vine's Complete Expository Dictionary of Old and New Testament Words defines the Hebrew word for sin (*awen*) as "iniquity [not being equal], vanity, sorrow, the absence of all that has true worth; hence it would denote 'morale worthlessness,' as in the actions of wrongdoing, evil devising, or false speaking."

In Adam's act of disobedience, Adam stepped away from being like God; no longer equal. Adam no longer relied on God for protection, for wisdom, for covering. Adam relied on Adam. Adam separated his path from God's.

Vine shows the Greek word for sin (*hamaria*) as "a missing of the mark." The imagery is like an archery contest. The archer's eye is on the target. The arrow is loosed. And, somewhere in the flight, the arrow changes course, missing the target. Sin.

Sin came into this world through the selfish action of one man. In Genesis 2, God told Adam to eat of every tree except the Tree of the Knowledge of Good and Evil. In Genesis 3, Adam did not confront the serpent or correct Eve as to what God had actually said. Eve ate and gave some also to Adam, who was with her. The Bible implies that during Eve's entire conversation with the serpent Adam was with his wife Eve. He did not stop her or correct her understanding of what God had said. Adam watched as Eve was led into deception and did nothing. When she ate, she turned to her husband who was right there with her, and Adam ate too.

Adam knew what God had said. Adam knew the price of sin, his sin. Adam chose to separate himself from God. Adam, who was surrounded by the presence of God, separated himself from God's presence to know the difference between good and evil. Adam chose to be separate from God. Being made in the image and likeness of God, Adam chose to no longer be like God. Adam chose to no longer have equity with God, equality with God, and chose inequality or iniquity. Adam chose sin. Adam, by choosing a different path than walking with God, missed the mark of a life in right relationship with God. Adam chose sin.

It was not God's plan that Man should be separate from God. God had made Man in His image and likeness, in the image and likeness of God[3]. Adam chose his own way over God's. Just as God had said, Adam died that day. He was torn from eternal life to a life in the flesh and a hope that in the judgment of God there would be a

---

[3] Genesis 1.26

deliverer: one who would come who would crush the head of the serpent yet bruise his heel[4]. God had to cover the sin of Adam, the missing of the mark of all Adam's descendants. Adam set the pattern of disobedience to the Word of God. In Genesis 3 when confronted by God, Adam cast the blame on Eve- the female God gave Adam, his wife and partner in life, the person who was to help him meet life's challenges. Eve follows the example of her husband. Eve now has the pattern and casts the blame on the serpent. Willful disobedience combined with denial of the act has become the pattern established. No care was given as to the consequences of the act of disobedience. All sin can be tied to willful disobedience, denial, and blame casting.

Man's first actions, after his willful disobedience, were to cover himself with fig leaves and hide. It is interesting that Adam used leaves to form his covering. Once the leaves are pulled from the branches, they begin to die. They may be green for a while, but they are dead and will wither. God interceded on behalf of Adam and Eve. God showed them how to make coverings for themselves out of animal hides. God shed blood to cover them.

---

[4] Genesis 3.15

As blood was spilled in the flesh to cover Adam and Eve[5], so too blood, a sacrifice, had to be spilled to cover Man in the spiritual. The blood sacrifices made by Man were a type of covering sacrifice. The only way to permanently cover the sin of Man was through a more perfect sacrifice, once for all.

"But in those sacrifices there is a reminder of sins year by year. For it is impossible for the blood of bulls and goats to take away sins. Therefore, when He comes into the world, He says, 'Sacrifice and offering Thou hast not desired, but a body Thou hast prepared for Me; in whole burnt offerings and sacrifices for sin Thou hast taken no pleasure.' Then I said, 'Behold, I have come (in the roll of the book it is written of Me) to do Thy will, O God.'
"After saying, above, 'Sacrifices and offerings and whole burnt offerings and sacrifices for sin Thou hast not desired, nor hast Thou taken pleasure in them,' (which are offered according to the Law), then He said, 'Behold I have come to do Thy will,' He takes away the first in order to establish the second. By this will we have been sanctified through the offering of the body of Jesus Christ once for all." –Hebrews 10.3-10 NAS

---

[5] Genesis 3.21

Jesus Christ became the vehicle of redemption for Man. A cost had to be attached to the sin of Man. A price had to be paid to bridge the separation of God and Man. Man had to be redeemed.

Redemption comes from the Latin word *redemptio*, meaning a buying back. Redemption is a variation of the English word redeem.

Redeem comes from the Latin word *redimere*, meaning to buy back or ransom. *Dimere* means to purchase. *Re* means back.

We can say the redemption Jesus Christ gave us at the cross was a buying back of Man from a price already paid. We who are in Christ Jesus have been valued twice: once at the creation of Man in the image and likeness of God, and the second at the cross.

The English word *redeem* comes from the root word *"deem"*, meaning to judge. We can also say that we have been re-judged for our sin and Jesus Christ took our place in judgment, paid the value to redeem. Jesus was punished under the judgment meant for us. He paid the price, the cost, of our judgment.

"Surely he hath borne our griefs, and carried our sorrows: yet we did esteem him stricken, smitten of God, and afflicted. But he was wounded for our transgressions, he was bruised for our iniquities:

the chastisement of our peace was upon him; and with his stripes we are healed." –Isaiah 53.4-5 KJV

Jesus redeemed us in his trials from the garden of Gethsemane, to false arrest and accusations, to mockings and beatings for serving God and Man, to trial and judgment, to ridicule and death sentence, to the shame of the cross, to suffering on our behalf, to receiving our judgment in his body, and to the separation from the Father and death. It was finished.

The entire price that needed to be paid was met at the cross when Jesus said it was finished[6]. The walls of separation were no longer there. The curtain separating the inner temple from innermost part was torn in two[7]. What hid the Holy of Holies from Man was no longer there. Man had access to God again. Now, there was no longer a need for anything to separate God from Man, except Man.

---

[6] John 19.30
[7] Matthew 15.38

5 | At: The "A" in Grace

Within the court system of the United States of America, if you are found guilty of your crime (sin), you are judged and must pay out the righteous requirements of that judgment, whatever it is. The guilty person disobeyed the law, broke covenant, and is required to make restitution for the crime.

The same is true of our relationship with God. The first judgment was at Adam. Even though sin had separated God from right fellowship with Man, it did not stop God from having conversations with Man. God warned Cain that sin was waiting for him at the door[8]. Cain did not heed God and sinned against his brother by killing him[9], and there was additional judgment.

At judgment, someone had to pay for the cost of restitution. Someone had to be judged and punished for the sin of Adam and all the descendents from Adam and Eve. Each one of us have been given the same choice, do what is right in the sight of God or to do what is right in our own understanding. In each instance, the descendants of Man have failed.

As the sin was a spiritual sin acted out in the natural, a natural act had to be performed to repair the spiritual breech between God and Man.

Paul, in his letter to the Romans, tells us that all have sinned and have fallen short (sin, missed the mark) of the glory of God[10]. All are guilty of sin.

In Genesis 2.17, God tells Adam the punishment for being judged disobedient. "…for in the day that you eat from it, you shall surely die."

The punishment was death. Just as the leaves Adam used to cloth himself were dead but still green for a little while. Adam, according to the

---

[8] Genesis 4.6
[9] Genesis 4.8
[10] Romans 3.23

Bible, lived 930 years and died. Remember, God is the Eternal, Self-Existent One in Whom all power exists. God made Man in His own image. Adam was no longer like God and died.

Since Adam failed to walk uprightly, circumspectly, and righteously with God, someone was needed who would, who could. As that spiritual perfection in right standing with God was lost, the breech demanded spiritual perfection, right standing with God, to repair that breech. As Adam was right with God before sin, God required another who was right with Him without the sin of separation from His will. The righteous requirement of spiritual law required a new Man. Jesus was that new Man, the last Adam, born of a woman, not descended from Man, but created by the Holy Spirit as with the first Adam.

The judgment and punishment for the "sin" had to fall on someone. Either the person committing the sin or someone else is required to take the sinner's place. Just as the Hebrew law placed the sin of the people on a goat and it was released into wilderness and judgment, so was a person righteous before God to take the sin of Man. The Bible says that such a person was and is the Messiah (Anointed One, Christ). Specifically, the one anointed to be the salvation of God's people.

King David of Israel most notably described the Anointed One[11] (Messiah) and the prophet Isaiah as receiving punishment[12].

It was at the cross where Jesus traded places in judgment. Through his life Jesus was perfect toward the Law and perfect toward God, his Father. Deuteronomy points out that if someone is worthy of death, he is put on a tree and a curse rests on him[13].

The wages of sin is death[14], a capital punishment. Our punishment was put on him[15]. Our sin was put on him. Jesus was put on a tree, a cross, for our sin to take our curse, our just punishment.

"For he hath made him to be sin for us, who knew no sin; that we might be made the righteousness of God in him."
- II Corinthians 5.18 KJV

---

[11] Psalm 2
[12] Isaiah 53
[13] Genesis 21.22-23
[14] Romans 6.23
[15] Romans 3.25

6 | Christ: The "C" in Grace

Who was this Christ, Messiah, Anointed One? What is the Christ? Why did it have to be Jesus? What does it mean to be "anointed?" First, what does the word "Christ" mean? The English word *christ* is very nearly a direct transliteration of the Greek word *christos*. The word *christos* came from the Greek verb *chriein*, to anoint. Therefore, the word *christ* means one who is anointed or anointed one.

In the last 1900 years, the word *christ* has become synonymous with Jesus, the Lord's Anointed, the Christ. But, what did it mean to be anointed?

The English verb "anoint" means to pour oil upon; to smear or rub over with oil or ointment. Anoint also means to *consecrate* by the use of oil, a sacred rite of great antiquity. Monarchs, prelates, and priests were anointed as part of the consecration ceremonies. This custom is still used today.

Consecrate means to devote to a sacred or high purpose, to dedicate. Aaron, the brother of Moses, and his sons were anointed as priests in the service of the Lord in the Tabernacle[16]. Sacrifices unto God were anointed[17]. The Tabernacle, itself, was anointed[18]. God commanded Samuel to anoint Saul as king over Israel[19]. God commanded Samuel to anoint David as king over Israel[20].

By these few examples it is shown that people or things are anointed for specific use, entitled or commissioned for a specific purpose.

Throughout history, many have been anointed. All were anointed, commissioned to

---

[16] Exodus 28.40
[17] Exodus 29.36
[18] Exodus 40.9
[19] I Samuel 9.16; 15.1
[20] I Samuel 16.12-13

some specific purpose. It has been said by some that there have been many "*christs*". And, there have been. But, to what purpose have they been anointed? Only one throughout history has been anointed to be the salvation of God's people.

Only one throughout history has been anointed to be the salvation of God's people, to bring healing and righteousness, to take Man's sin and shame on himself, to be judged and take captivity captive, to rise again as high priest of a more perfect covenant. Jesus is his name.

From Genesis 3 through Malachi 3, the prophets spoke of only one who would repair the gap between God and Man. Jesus was that prophesied repairer of the breech and spiritual sacrifice. But, why did it have to be Jesus?

The English name *Jesus* comes from the Latin word *Iesus*, the Greek word *Iesous*, which comes from the Hebrew word *yeshua*, which is a contraction of the word *yehoshua*. *Yehoshua* comes from the two Hebrew words *YHWH* (God, Jehovah) and *hoshia* (to help). A literal translation of the name Jesus would be "God helps" or the "help of God."

Mary, the mother of Jesus, was told by Gabriel, the Angel of the Lord, what to name her son[21]. The person we have come to know as Jesus was to be the embodiment of the help of God; the help of God in human flesh.

Since sin entered into the world through a man created solely by God, a new man had to be created that was not tied to the inherited sin of Man. God, through Mary, created a new Adam, Jesus- the help of God.

Jesus grew to be a man, a righteous man, a man right with God. He never sinned. He was never separate from the will of God; His heart was fully toward, was righteous toward the Lord God.

In due time, Jesus was baptized by John, His cousin, in the Jordan River[22]. It was at that point the Lord God anointed Jesus when the Holy Spirit descended upon him in the form of a dove. Jesus was led from the Jordan to the desert and was tested there[23]. Jesus returned from the desert through Galilee to Nazareth and proclaimed to what purpose He was anointed[24]. Jesus fulfilled the prophecies concerning the Christ. But, why did the Savior have to be Jesus?

First, in Genesis 3, as part of God's judgment against the serpent, God foretold that it would be the seed of the woman that crushed the

---

[21] Luke 1.31
[22] Matthew 3.13-17; Luke 3.21-22; John 1.29-34
[23] Luke 4.1-13
[24] Luke 4.14-21

serpent[25]. The repairer of the breech would also be the vehicle of God's judgment.

In Deuteronomy 18, the Lord God said He would raise up a Prophet from the midst of the people and He would be like God and speak for God[26]. He would rule as King[27]. He would be a descendant of King David and a priest-king like Melchizedek[28]. He would be a sign to kings and the world. He would be a ruler[29]. He would be a greatly exalted sacrifice[30]. He would be God with us[31]. He would be the manifested Word of God as a Man[32]. He was from God and the Lamb of God[33]. He came to take away the sin of the world[34].

[25] Genesis 3.15
[26] Deuteronomy 18.15-19
[27] Psalm 2
[28] Psalm 110; Mark 12.35-73; Hebrews 6.20, 7.1-3, 8.1-6
[29] Isaiah 9.6-7
[30] Isa 52.13-15, 53.1-12
[31] Matthew 1.23
[32] John 1.1-14
[33] John 1.15-36
[34] John 1.29, 36

7 | Expense: The "E" in Grace

The expense. The cost. The price. The payment due for the judgment against the sin of Man. That is what Jesus came to earth to be. What did it cost Jesus to be our sin sacrifice, our payment for the judgment of sin?

Jesus was and is God. Isaiah 9.6 said His name would be called Mighty God, Eternal Father. His name would be Emmanuel, which is translated

God with us[35]. He was in the beginning with God and was God[36]. He was God become flesh[37]. In Him dwells the fullness of the Godhead bodily[38]. He enjoyed all of the fullness of God and all things came into being by Him. Apart from Him nothing came into being that has come into being[39]. He was God. He was and is the Eternal, Self-Existent One, in Whom all powers exist (*YHWH Elohim*). He gave up all of that to be our sacrifice, our replacement, our punishment, our judgment payment.

It should go without saying that being *YHWH Elohim* is the ultimate expression of wealth, power, and position. The creative God Who could make all He desires. Yet, though He was rich He became poor[40]. He traded His wealth, His riches, to be a righteous man before God.

Jesus walked in everyway as a man. He was born. He was hungry. He was dirty. He was hot. He was cold. He knew joy. He knew pain. He had to learn Hebrew and the Law. He had to learn carpentry. He had to deal with splinters and customers. He was a little boy. He was a teenager.

---

[35] Isaiah 9.6.-7; Matthew 1.23
[36] John 1.1-2
[37] John 1.14
[38] Colossians 2.9
[39] John 1.2
[40] II Corinthians 8.9

He was a young, successful businessman. He was a brother. He was a son. He was a relative. He did all as God commanded. He was led of the Spirit. He did not walk in the fullness of the Godhead. He was a man. He did everything as a man, except one thing. He did not sin. He was never separate from the will of God.

Going from knowing all, being able to do all you plan to do, to being human is poverty.

More was required of Jesus, the Man, the Son of God, than just walking through this life as a righteous man of God.

Under the Hebrew Law, on the Day of Atonement a spotless lamb was offered as a sin offering. This blood sacrifice covered the sin of Israel for the year. This sacrifice was done annually[41]. Jesus was to be an eternal replacement for the annual sacrifices[42].

Early in Jesus' preaching career He tried explaining to those around Him that He would be the Lamb that was slain for their sin[43] and crucified. Either they did not believe Him or their hearts were hardened against Him.

"If I told you earthly things and you do not believe, how shall you believe if I tell you

---

[41] Hebrews 9.7, 25, 10.1, 3-4
[42] Hebrews 9-10
[43] John 3.14, 8.27, 12.27

heavenly things? And no one has ascended into heaven, but He who descended from heaven, even the Son of man. And as Moses lifted up the serpent in the wilderness, even so must the Son of Man be lifted up; that whoever believes may in Him have eternal life. For God so loved the world that He gave His only begotten Son, that whoever believes in Him should not perish, but have eternal life. For God did not send the Son into the world to judge the world, but the world should be saved through Him." - John 3.12-17 NAS

Another cost to be paid was the cost of breaking covenant. In ancient times a covenant was a bonding agreement that could not be broken without a cost to the one breaking the covenant. The cost was agreed upon before the covenant was made. A blood covenant required the spilling of blood, the taking of a life, and the taking the life of the one breaking the covenant. God made a covenant in blood with Moses and the children of Israel. This blood covenant required the blood, the death, of the one breaking the covenant.

"For where a covenant (testament) is, there must of necessity be the death of the one who made it. For a covenant is valid only when men are dead, for it is never in force while the one who made it lives." - Hebrews 9.16-17 NAS

God's love for us was (is) so great that He, Himself, paid the cost of our covenant breaking and thereby created a new covenant.

"And for this reason He is the mediator of a new covenant, in order that since a death has taken place for the redemption of the transgressions that were committed under the first covenant, those who have been called may receive the promise of the eternal inheritance." - Hebrews 9.15 NAS

Not only did God make covenant, bless Man, forgive sin, but personally paid the price of the judgment of sin and the price of covenant breaking.

The Eternal, Self-Existent One, in Whom all powers exists (*YHWH Elohim*) took our punishment, was scorned, mocked, beaten, whipped with a Roman scourge, had his beard plucked, forced to wear a crown of thorns, judged falsely of blasphemy and sedition, forced to carry a cross timber down a street of deriders, nailed to a cross, left to suffocate on the cross, taunted by onlookers, received the punishment of our sins in His body, He was separated from God the Father and received death, unjustifiably.

The Eternal, Self-Existent One, in Whom all powers exists (*YHWH Elohim*) died that you might live. God separated Himself, in our sin, from all that was holy that we might be made holy.

He died that we might have life, riches, blessing, and right standing with God the Father and all that is holy if we only believe He paid it all on the cross at Golgotha[44]. How much more can you love someone than to punish yourself for the sin of your children?

The cost of sin was death. The price of redemption was equally death. It may seem harsh, but we are not just of this Earth. We are of God, made in His image and likeness, to be His children with Him. There was only one way He would allow us to be close to Him, and that was through Jesus, from the garden through the cross, through the grave to resurrection and ascension.

It cost God everything to give us the freedom of this grace from Jesus Christ.

---

[44] Matthew 26-27; Mark 14-15; John 18-19

8 | Receiving the Gift

It is clear to me that Man has been bought with an exceedingly high price. Yet God does not hold any animosity toward Man. In fact God has decided that due to Man's right relationship with Himself through belief in what Jesus Christ did for Man at the cross that God is satisfied.

Additionally, now that He has a right relationship with Man, God has decided He will richly bless Man with unmerited favor and every good gift.

"Blessed be the God and Father of our Lord Jesus Christ, who hath blessed us with all spiritual blessings in heavenly places in Christ. According as he hath chosen us in him before the foundation of the world, that we should be holy and without blame before him in love. Having predestinated us unto the adoption of children by Jesus Christ to himself according to the good pleasure of his will. To the praise of the glory of his grace, wherein he hath made us accepted in the beloved. In whom we have redemption through his blood, the forgiveness of sins, according to the riches of his grace." Ephesians 1.3-7 KJV

"But God, who is rich in mercy, for his great love wherewith he loved us, even when we were dead in sins hath quickened us together with Christ, (by grace ye are saved); and hath raised us up together, and made us sit together in heavenly places in Christ Jesus. That in the ages to come he might shew the exceeding riches of his grace in his kindness toward us through Christ Jesus. For by grace are ye saved through faith; and that not of yourselves: it is the gift of God." Ephesians 2.4-8 KJV

What is grace then? Grace is a free-will gift of love from an Everlasting, Eternal, Self-Existent

God who loves Man so greatly as to punish Himself rather than His children. All that He requires is that we love Him, trust Him, and obey Him. It is much like me telling my son in his toddler years to not touch something because it is hot and I get burned in the process. And, all I tell my son is don't do that you will get burned.

Jesus took my place. He was burned in my stead. The chastisement of my peace was upon Him. By the stripes He received I am made whole.[45] The grace He gives us is this. We can walk with Him in the cool of the day just as if we never sinned, just as if this was the way it always was.

Grace is His bearing me up when life is difficult. Grace is two sets of footprints in the sand when I need a friend and one set when I can no longer bear up because He carries me.

Grace is not a thing to be possessed or demanded. Grace is the free gift of His good pleasure in acts designed to assist and bless Man. Grace is not a substance. Grace is an action from a loving Father who is God. And, the only way into this grace with the Father is through the selfless sacrifice of Jesus Christ, the Son, at the cross.

Man cannot come near unto God without first accepting the price paid by Jesus Christ. All

---

[45] Isaiah 53

must accept that Jesus paid the price, was Man's judgment sacrifice, once for all- if Man only believes.

Simply pray and mean it from your heart, your inward self:

Jesus, I believe you are God. I believe you are the Son of God and the Son of Man. I accept the price you paid for me at the cross. I ask you to come live with me. Be Emmanuel, God with me. Let me receive your grace. Forgive me of my sins that I might live with you all ways. Lord Jesus, be Lord of my life. Let my life be an offering pleasing to you. Let me experience the grace You paid so high of a price to give me. Come abide with me and let me abide with You. Let me dwell in Your house forever. Amen.

9 | What to do next?

After having received the grace of the Lord Jesus Christ, you can begin building a relationship with your heavenly Father.

Get into a Bible-believing, Bible-teaching church. Get around other believers; get fed the word of God, and fellowship with your family in Christ. Learn of God.

Begin developing a history with God. Commune with Him; that simply means start having a conversation with Him expecting Him to participate. He will.

Get yourself a good Bible. Pick a translation that makes sense to you. It does not necessarily need to be the King James Version. And, read it. Meditate on it. Ask God questions regarding what you read and expect Him to show you answers. He will. If any ask of Him wisdom He will give it[46].

After the Grace of the Lord Jesus Christ has been received you have access to all the fullness of God the Father. There is now no separation for Man and God. You just have to learn to live in a right relationship with God; and this only by renewing your mind through God's Word, both written and spoken, and choosing to walk with Him.

As with the prodigal son returning to his father's house, once you have received the price paid at the cross by Jesus, you now have access to all that is in your Father's house. You are family. All of the other graces, gifts, and good things are yours to enjoy.

Now comes the time to learn what gifts there are from God for you to enjoy.

---

[46] James 1.5

Appendix

Bibliography

* King James Version, English translation of the Holy Bible, c.1611 (KJV)
* New American Standard Bible translation of the Holy Bible
  * ©1997 The Lockman Foundation
* New Strong's Dictionary of Hebrew and Greek Words; ISBN 0-917006-01-1
* Vine's Complete Expository Dictionary of Old and New Testament Words
  * Copyright 1985
  * ISBN 0-8407-7559-8
* Webster's New Twentieth Century Dictionary – Unabridged
  * Copyright 1983
  * ISBN 0-671-41819-X

Do You Know Jesus?

You can know Jesus and the Creator of the universe. The God of the Bible wants to live with you, wants to be a part of your life, and wants you to be a part of His life. The thing that separates you from Him is sin. Sin is those acts or choices that lead you away from a life with God. God changed all of that with His son Jesus.

Jesus came to this world to save those who would believe on him. Jesus said he was the way, the truth, and the life; that no one could come to the Father – God in Heaven – without coming first to Jesus.

You can have the relationship right now. Only believe. Believe down in your heart of hearts that God is able to save you from the judgment to come. Everyone will be judged on how they lived their lives. It is not about being a good person. It is about your relationship with God as your Father.

Simply Pray:

Jesus, I want to know you. Come into my life. Show me the Father God. Let me get to know you. Forgive me my sin, my trespasses, the errors of my ways against you. I ask you now to live with me, be with me, and lead me in a life with you. I receive your grace –your gift of forgiveness. Send me you Holy Spirit. Lead me in the way I should go. Amen.

About the Author

Dr. David J Rogers is an author, teacher, and minister of the Gospel of Jesus Christ. He is a learner, a well-rounded teacher, and dynamic speaker. He works with ministry organizations in teaching, in ministry, in pastoral care, and in support roles.

...

www.docrogerswrites.com

...

A portion of the proceeds from the sale of this book will go to missions and to preach the gospel.

Made in the USA
Columbia, SC
10 August 2024